J   4533215H
550   Asimov, Isaac, 1920-
ASI   Earth

W9-AQZ-838

RD

HICKORY FLAT PUBLIC LIBRARY
2740 EAST CHEROKEE DRIVE
CANTON, GEORGIA 30115

SEQUOYAH REGIONAL LIBRARY

3 8749 0045 3321 5

Isaac Asimov's 21st Century Library of the Universe

Library of the Universe

The Solar System

Earth

BY ISAAC ASIMOV
WITH REVISIONS AND UPDATING BY RICHARD HANTULA

THIS BOOK IS THE PROPERTY OF
SEQUOYAH REGIONAL LIBRARY
CANTON, GEORGIA

Gareth Stevens Publishing
A WORLD ALMANAC EDUCATION GROUP COMPANY

Please visit our web site at: www.garethstevens.com
For a free color catalog describing Gareth Stevens Publishing's list of high-quality
books and multimedia programs, call 1-800-542-2595 (USA) or 1-800-387-3178 (Canada).
Gareth Stevens Publishing's fax: (414) 332-3567.

The reproduction rights to all photographs and illustrations in this book are controlled by the individuals
or institutions credited on page 32 and may not be reproduced without their permission.

Library of Congress Cataloging-in-Publication Data

Asimov, Isaac.
    Earth / by Isaac Asimov; with revisions and updating by Richard Hantula.
       p. cm. — (Isaac Asimov's 21st century library of the universe. The solar system)
    Rev. ed. of: Our planet Earth. 1995.
    Summary: A description of Earth, the third planet from the sun, which includes information
on its origins, composition, and unique characteristics.
    Includes bibliographical references and index.
    ISBN 0-8368-3234-5 (lib. bdg.)
    1. Earth—Juvenile literature. [1. Earth.] I. Hantula, Richard. II. Asimov, Isaac. Our planet
Earth. III. Title. IV. Isaac Asimov's 21st century library of the universe. Solar system.
QB631.4.A86   2002
550—dc21   2002066919

This edition first published in 2002 by
Gareth Stevens Publishing
A World Almanac Education Group Company
330 West Olive Street, Suite 100
Milwaukee, WI 53212 USA

Revised and updated edition © 2002 by Gareth Stevens, Inc. Original edition published in 1988
by Gareth Stevens, Inc. under the title *Earth: Our Home Base.* Second edition published in 1995
by Gareth Stevens, Inc. under the title *Our Planet Earth.* Text © 2002 by Nightfall, Inc. End
matter and revisions © 2002 by Gareth Stevens, Inc.

Series editor: Betsy Rasmussen
Cover design and layout adaptation: Melissa Valuch
Picture research: Kathy Keller
Additional picture research: Diane Laska-Swanke
Artwork commissioning: Kathy Keller and Laurie Shock
Production director: Susan Ashley

The editors at Gareth Stevens Publishing have selected science author Richard Hantula to bring
this classic series of young people's information books up to date. Richard Hantula has written
and edited books and articles on science and technology for more than two decades. He was
the senior U.S. editor for the *Macmillan Encyclopedia of Science.*

In addition to Hantula's contribution to this most recent edition, the editors would like to
acknowledge the participation of two noted science authors, Greg Walz-Chojnacki and
Francis Reddy, as contributors to earlier editions of this work.

All rights to this edition reserved to Gareth Stevens, Inc. No part of this book may be reproduced,
stored in a retrieval system, or transmitted in any form or by any means, electronic, mechanical,
photocopying, recording, or otherwise, without the prior written permission of the publisher except
for the inclusion of brief quotations in an acknowledged review.

Printed in the United States of America

1 2 3 4 5 6 7 8 9 06 05 04 03 02

Contents

We live in an enormously large place – the Universe. It is only natural that we would want to understand this place, so scientists and engineers have developed instruments and spacecrafts that have told us far more about the Universe than we could possibly imagine.

We have seen planets up close, and spacecrafts have even landed on some. We have learned about quasars and pulsars, super-novas and colliding galaxies, and black holes and dark matter. We have gathered amazing data about how the Universe may have come into being and how it may end. Nothing could be more astonishing.

In all the unbelievably vast Universe, there is only one world that we call home, where the drama of life as we know it began. That world is Earth. Earth is just one small planet circling one middle-sized star in a corner of a single, unremarkable galaxy. It is an incredibly fascinating place, however, filled with marvels and miracles.

• Earth •

Above: An artist's conception of what the beginning of our Solar System looked like. Planets form in the swirling disk of gas and dust surrounding the newborn Sun.

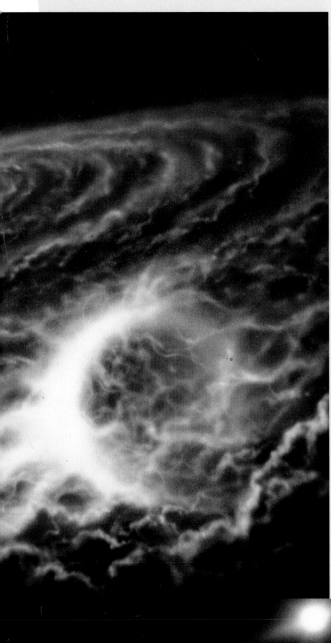

Earth's Beginning

Scientists think that nearly five billion years ago, a vast cloud of dust and gas was slowly swirling in space. The cloud's gravitational pull forced the particles of dust and gas tighter and tighter together. As the cloud grew smaller, it whirled faster and grew hotter at its center.

Beyond the center of the cloud, the dust and gas built up and formed rocks and boulders. The very center of the cloud became so hot that a star developed – our Sun.

Meanwhile, the rocks and boulders gradually came together with leftover gas to make the planets of our Solar System. One of the planets that formed was our Earth.

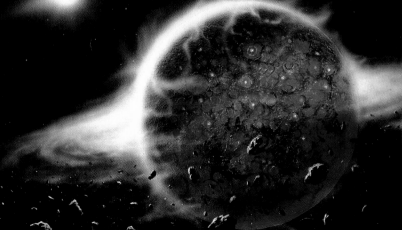

Right: The young Earth sweeps up some of the rocky leftovers of the Solar System's birth.

5

Earth Takes Shape

Earth was quite hot as it formed, but it gradually became cooler. Gases and water that were trapped in the rocks slowly fizzed out, producing Earth's atmosphere and vast oceans.

Slowly, the heaviest materials — metals, such as iron and nickel — settled to Earth's center and melted to form a hot metal core. Around the core, a rocky mantle of solid matter took shape. The mantle is hot enough to be slightly soft. The rock in the mantle slowly moves.

After Earth had already taken shape, the last pieces of rock to join it left marks where they hit the planet's surface. These marks are called craters. Craters made by such impacts in the early years of Earth's history were gradually erased by wind, water, or hot liquid rock from volcanoes. In more recent periods, Earth has been hit much more rarely by large pieces of rock from space, but large impacts still occur every once in a while, producing craters. If the craters were not made long enough ago to be erased by now, their remains can still be seen.

Right: Glowing as it travels through the atmosphere, rocky debris crashes onto the young Earth's hot surface.

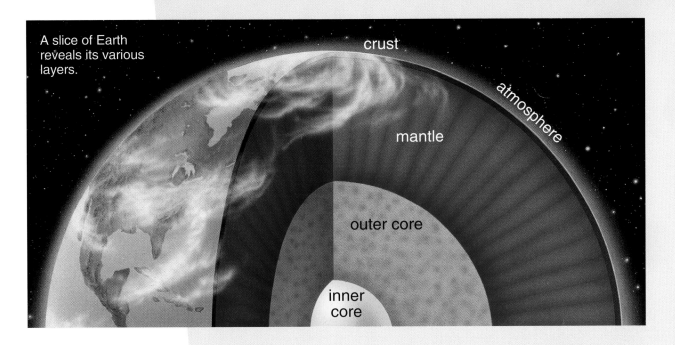

A slice of Earth reveals its various layers.

crust

atmosphere

mantle

outer core

inner core

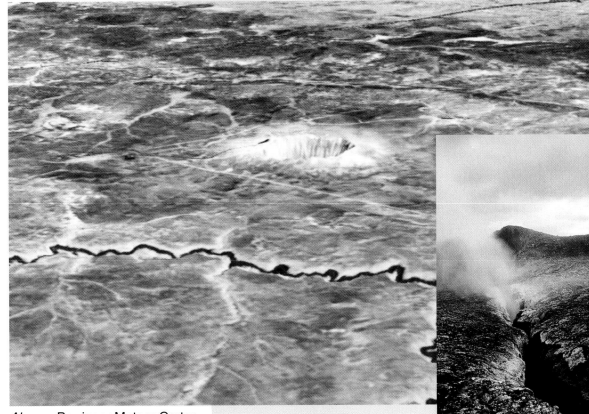

Above: Barringer Meteor Crater in Arizona.

Right: Even today, gases escape from within our planet.

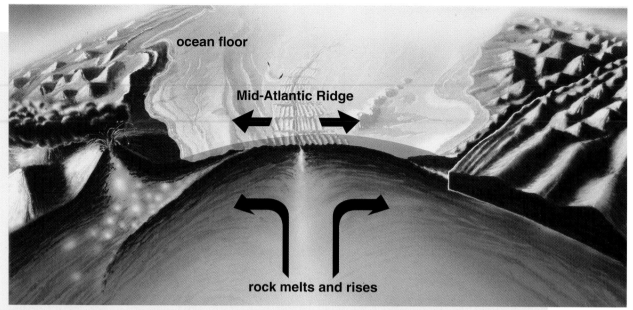

Above: Hot rock from deep within our Earth builds mountains as the ocean floor spreads apart.

Above: Earth's longest mountain range lies mostly under the water. This "mid-oceanic ridge" circles Earth and is about 50,000 miles (80,000 kilometers) in length. The portion known as the Mid-Atlantic Ridge divides the Atlantic Ocean down the middle.

Constantly Changing Earth

Earth's crust is not one solid shell. It is broken into many pieces called plates. These plates move slowly and steadily, constantly changing the surface of Earth.

Many scientists think that about 200 million to 300 million years ago, the Earth had a single supercontinent called Pangea, which combined all the major landmasses. As Earth's wandering plates continued to move, Pangea slowly rifted apart, and the continents we know today began to take shape.

Where Earth's plates pull apart, hot rock comes up from below and forms mountains in the middle of ocean floors. This is one way islands develop. Some ocean islands are simply the tops of such underwater mountains — the Azores in the Atlantic Ocean are an example.

Left: Earth looked quite different hundreds of millions of years ago. At one time, many scientists think all the major land areas were joined together in one giant continent called Pangea.

Our Earth — what a wonderful world!

Earth's oceans are much larger than Earth's continents. Europe, Asia, and Africa, for example, have a combined area of 33 million square miles (85 million square kilometers), but the Pacific Ocean alone is 64 million square miles (166 million sq km). If you count the other oceans, seas, gulfs, and bays, about 71 percent of Earth's surface is covered with water.

Mountains and Earthquakes

While the plates are pulling apart in some places, they are coming together in other places. This collision of plates can cause the crust to crumple and can give rise to earthquakes.

Tens of millions of years ago, India "bumped" into Asia, and the crumpling of the crust created the Himalaya Mountains. The Rocky Mountains in North America were created by the collision of the Pacific and North American plates.

Sometimes, the plates rub past one another. When this happens, the plates do not slide smoothly. They jerk along, under great tension. We feel this as an earthquake. The boundaries of the sliding plates are marked by faults, or cracks, across Earth's surface.

Earthquakes can reshape the land and topple buildings, such as these in San Francisco in 1989 (*right*) and Los Angeles in 1994 (*opposite, top*).

Mt. Everest — just a sinking sensation?

Earth's oceans are deeper than its mountains are high. The highest mountain on Earth is Mt. Everest. Its peak is 29,035 feet (8,849.9 meters) above sea level. At a place in the Pacific Ocean called the Challenger Deep, the ocean floor is 36,198 feet (11,033 m) below sea level. If Mt. Everest could be placed into the Challenger Deep, the entire mountain would disappear with plenty of room to spare!

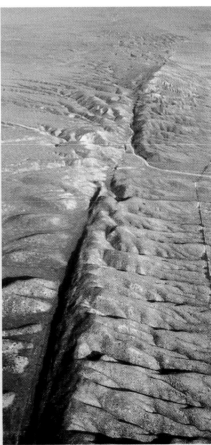

Right: The San Andreas Fault in California. Pressure builds up as plates try to grind past each other. When the rocks give way, an earthquake occurs.

Above: Mt. Everest, the highest mountain on Earth, rises in the eastern Himalayas between Nepal and Tibet.

In 1991, Mt. Pinatubo in the Philippines had its first major eruption in over 600 years.

Volcanoes

Volcanoes are found not only at the mid-oceanic ridge where plates are separating but also in places where two plates collide and one of them slides under the other. As the plate sinks, its rock is heated to the melting point. Some of this melted rock makes its way upward and produces volcanoes.

Most of the ocean floor beneath the Pacific is one big plate. All around its edge, there are volcanoes and earthquakes, so the edge is called the Ring of Fire. One of the biggest eruptions in the Ring of Fire in recent years occurred in 1991 at a volcano in the Philippines named Mt. Pinatubo. The volcano shot a cloud of ash as high as 25 miles (40 km) into the air.

Volcanoes may also occur in the middle of a plate if the plate happens to be passing over a spot in the mantle where hot melted rock is rising. An example is the volcano called Kilauea in Hawaii. It sometimes releases a stream of melted rock, or lava, forming a river of fire.

Above: The volcano Paricutín in Mexico started as a smoking crack in a cornfield in 1943. A volcanic cone quickly developed, reaching a height of about 460 feet (140 m) in the first week. Within a year, it destroyed two villages and grew to over 1,500 feet (450 m) high.

The island that exploded

The greatest volcanic eruption in modern times took place in 1883 on a little Indonesian island called Krakatau, which was actually a volcano. The eruption created huge waves of water that drowned some 34,000 people. Another 2,000 or more were killed by flows of hot ash. One of the explosions produced by the eruption was so loud that it could be heard 3,000 miles (4,800 km) away. Rocks were hurled miles into the air. Luckily, volcanoes rarely explode so violently.

Earth's Active Atmosphere

Earth is surrounded by a vast amount of air. At first, this atmosphere was made up of nitrogen and carbon dioxide. As simple forms of life developed, they changed the carbon dioxide to oxygen. This made it possible for people and animals to breathe. In turn, when people and animals exhale, or breathe out, they return carbon dioxide to the air.

The atmosphere is unevenly heated by the Sun. Warm air rises and cold air sinks. This sets up a movement that creates the winds. When ocean water evaporates, it cools and is changed into clouds in the upper air. The clouds are made of water droplets. Eventually, the water returns to Earth in the form of rain. Sometimes, the combination of water and wind can result in violent storms, such as hurricanes and tornadoes.

Below: Earth's atmosphere was not always as welcoming to living things as it is in present times.

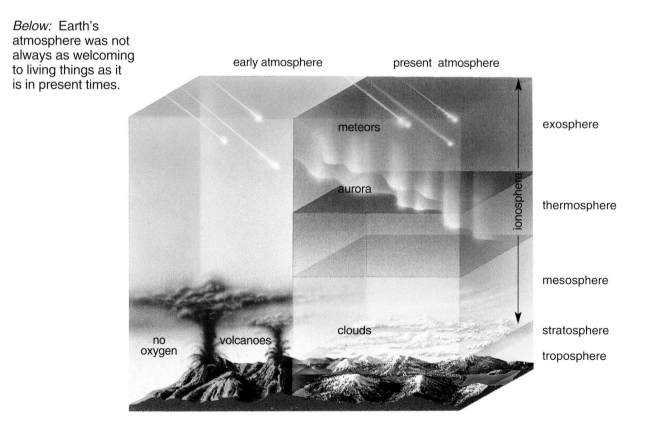

early atmosphere

present atmosphere

meteors

aurora

clouds

no oxygen

volcanoes

exosphere

ionosphere

thermosphere

mesosphere

stratosphere

troposphere

Thunderstorms bring strong winds and lightning — even hurricanes and tornadoes.

Right: Plants use the gases people and animals exhale to make their food — and to make the oxygen people and animals need to breathe.

15

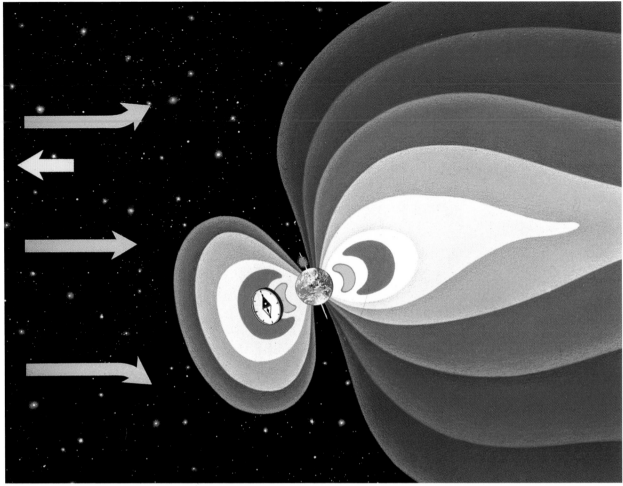

Above: Particles from the distant Sun *(unseen, at left)* pull and stretch Earth's magnetic field. Most of the particles flow around the magnetic field, but some of them become trapped inside it. These particles usually enter the atmosphere over Earth's poles.

Right: Auroras can be as colorful as a rainbow, but they are usually green or blue-green.

Earth's Magnetic Attraction

As Earth turns, the melted iron within its central core swirls. The swirling iron sets up a magnetic field that surrounds Earth. This makes Earth a gigantic magnet. This magnetism allows compasses to work. Compass needles continually point toward Earth's magnetic poles.

The Sun is always giving off particles that have electric charges. This is called the solar wind. The solar wind could harm life on Earth, but it becomes trapped in Earth's magnetic field before it can reach us. At Earth's polar regions, however, some of the particles do reach our

Above: When solar particles collide with gases in Earth's atmosphere, the gas atoms give off light. This phenomenon is called an aurora.

atmosphere. This makes the atmosphere glow in a spectacular sight called the aurora.

Earth's magnetic field — time for a change?

Earth's magnetic field sometimes weakens, reverses itself, and then grows stronger. If this happened today, a compass that was pointing north would begin to point south. Scientists know that Earth has had many magnetic reversals, although the last one happened 750,000 to 780,000 years ago. No one knows how or why reversals occur. Earth's magnetic field has been getting weaker since at least the mid-19th century. If this continues, it will have no strength at all in about 1,300 years. Perhaps there is a magnetic reversal coming up.

Understanding Our World Through Others

What we learn about other worlds can help us understand our own.

Like Earth, Mars has polar ice caps, and each day is about 24 hours long. Mars is also much colder than Earth. Venus has a thicker cloud layer and atmosphere than Earth. The Great Red Spot on Jupiter is really a giant storm – like a hurricane that seems to go on forever. Jupiter's moon Io has spectacular volcanic eruptions. Our Moon has no liquid water, almost no atmosphere, and has changed very little over time. By studying the Moon closely, scientists can discover what the Solar System was like in its early days.

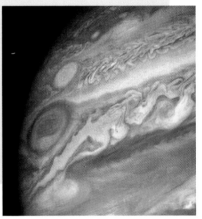

Above: The Great Red Spot, a storm much larger than Earth, has been seen on Jupiter since the invention of the telescope in 1608.

A June 2001 Hubble Space telescope image of Mars with polar caps (described as the best view of Mars ever obtained from Earth).

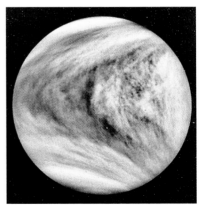

Above: Thick clouds mask the surface of Venus.

Above: Astronauts have been able to watch Earth rise over the Moon's surface.

Above: The plume of an erupting volcano rises over Io, a moon of Jupiter.

Above: Mars, the fourth planet from the Sun, is too cold to sustain life as we know it. Venus, the second planet from the Sun, is too hot. Earth, in between, has just the right conditions for life.

Above: Humans share the planet with a great variety of other life-forms, such as the lemon butterfly fish of Hawaii.

Earth – A Very Special World

Although other planets in our Solar System can help us learn about Earth, our planet is still quite different from any of the other planets.

Other planets are either too small to hold a substantial atmosphere, or their surface is too hot or too cold for water to stay liquid. Earth has an ocean of water that is needed for life, as we know it, to develop. Earth is just the right size and temperature for life to flourish.

There might be other worlds like Earth circling some stars, but we do not yet know anything about them.

Deep freeze or hothouse?

Just 10,000 years ago, enormous sheets of ice covered Canada, Scandinavia, and the northern parts of Siberia and the United States. Many scientists think that ice ages come and go because very small changes in Earth's orbit around the Sun cause changes in the amount of heat different areas of our planet receive from the Sun. On the other hand, many scientists are concerned that human activities will make the planet warmer over the next few decades. Both theories may be right – depending on how far into the future you look.

Our Fragile Planet

In future times, Earth might not have ideal conditions for life. The heat we receive from the Sun, for example, could change, so that a new ice age starts. Actions by humans also affect the conditions for life on Earth. Our population is ever-increasing. Right now, there are more than 6 billion of us. We need space and materials, so we cut down forests, driving some forms of life into extinction. As a result of human activity, chemicals that may be dangerous to living things get into rivers, lakes, oceans, and the atmosphere. Chemicals released into the atmosphere by humans are making the ozone layer thinner. This layer keeps certain harmful radiation produced by the Sun from reaching Earth's surface.

Wildlife is affected by the actions of humans.

Left: This gull died as a result of becoming trapped in a plastic beverage ring.

Right: A dolphin lost its life after accidentally becoming entangled in a fishing net.

There's a hole in our ozone!

Certain chemicals that have been used in air conditioners, spray cans, and other products contain chlorine that can damage the protective layer of ozone in Earth's atmosphere. Ozone is a form of oxygen, and this layer is about 12 to 30 miles (19 to 48 km) above Earth's surface. Even there, ozone exists only in small amounts, but it serves to shield Earth from the Sun's most harmful ultraviolet light. Studies have shown that in recent years, the ozone over Antarctica has become very thin each spring. Scientists named this area the "ozone hole." Similar thinning has been seen over the Arctic. International agreements have put some limits on the use of ozone-destroying chemicals, but so far they have not eliminated it.

Above and below: The world's rain forests are shrinking, as humans burn or cut down trees in order to use the land for various purposes.

Above: Air pollution from smokestacks.

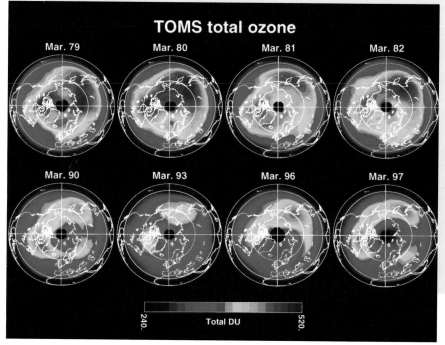

TOMS total ozone

Mar. 79 Mar. 80 Mar. 81 Mar. 82

Mar. 90 Mar. 93 Mar. 96 Mar. 97

240. Total DU 520.

Left: The ozone hole over Antarctica has gotten bigger in recent years. As the amount of damaging chlorine in the atmosphere increases, the amount of protective ozone decreases. TOMS ozone series from NASA shows the long-term situation of the ozone hole over Antarctica.

A view of Earth made by Defense Meteorological Satellite, showing city lights.

The Worlds Beyond

Russian scientist and rocket pioneer Konstantin Tsiolkovsky said, "Earth is humanity's cradle, but you can't stay in the cradle forever."

In 1969, a human stepped on the Moon for the first time in history. So far, a total of twelve people have walked on the Moon. Scientists are making plans for humans to visit Mars some day. One day, there may be entire cities in space, where thousands of people will make their homes.

That is all in the future. Meanwhile, we have placed space stations in orbit around Earth where a few astronauts and scientists can live and do research. The first expandable space station, called *Mir*, was built by the former Soviet Union. It orbited Earth from 1986 to 2001. Construction of an *International Space Station*, sponsored by the United States and other countries, began in 1998 when the first section was launched by Russia.

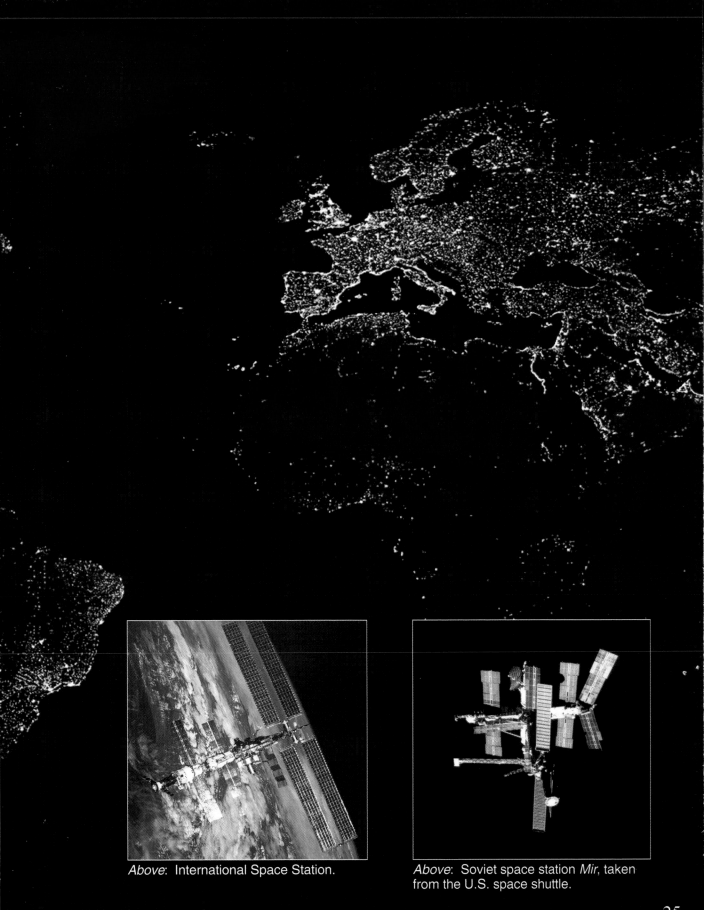

Above: International Space Station.

Above: Soviet space station *Mir*, taken from the U.S. space shuttle.

Terraforming Other Worlds

People may one day live in domed cities on the Moon and Mars. People could also live underneath the ground on these new worlds. It might even be possible to bring water and oxygen to Mars and make the conditions there similar to Earth's. We might be able to take some of the carbon dioxide away from Venus and add oxygen. That would cool Venus, which is now too hot for life as we know it.

Terraforming other planets, or making them like Earth, is something that we might be able to do in the future. The day may even come when we can visit the stars. We might discover planets so similar to Earth that they will not need terraforming!

For now, Earth's future is our future. Let's take good care of our Earth.

Right: As we travel to other worlds, we might try to change their climates to suit human life. Perhaps the Sun will one day peek through the thick clouds of Venus to shine on a beach filled with vacationers.

We are just beginning to explore the possibilities of permanent human habitation in space.

Earth

The Sun and its Solar System
(*left to right*): Mercury, Venus,
Earth, Mars, Jupiter, Saturn,
Uranus, Neptune, Pluto.

Earth's Moon

Diameter	Average Distance from Earth's Center	Percentage of Earth's Diameter
2,159 miles (3,475 km)	238,900 miles (384,400 km)	27%

Compared to What We Think Is Big on Earth,

Earth Is . . .

• **so wide** that if you could drill a giant hole through it and fill the hole with the world's tallest building, you could stuff 28,220 of the structures into the hole and still not have anything sticking out. The twin Petronas Towers in Kuala Lampur, Malaysia, rank as the world's tallest building with a height of 1,483 feet (452 meters).

• **so big** around that if you could drive around the world at 55 miles (88.5 km) an hour without stopping, it would take you about 453 hours before you returned from where you started. That is almost 19 days of nonstop driving!

But Earth Is Also:

• **so tiny** compared to the Sun that you could stuff more than a million Earths in the space the Sun takes up!

• **so far away from Mars** that it would take you about a year to get there and another year to come back!

• **our little planet.** As any astronomer or astronaut can tell you, our little planet takes up just a speck in space, but that little speck is where we live — and the place from which we can study the rest of our vast Universe.

Above: A close-up of Earth and its lone moon. Our Moon is a little over ¹/₄ as wide as Earth, so the two could be thought of as a double planet.

Fact File: Our Special Home — Earth

Earth is the fifth-largest known planet in our Solar System and the third-closest to the Sun. It is the largest of the inner planets — just over 7,926 miles (12,756 km) wide at its equator. This means that our planet is about five percent bigger than Venus, almost twice the diameter of Mars, and more than 2.5 times the diameter of Mercury.

Earth is also the heaviest inner planet of our Solar System. It weighs about 6.58 sextillion tons (5.97 sextillion metric tons).

It is about 23 percent heavier than Venus, 9.3 times heavier than Mars, and more than 18 times the mass of Mercury.

Earth, however, is still only a speck when compared with even an average star, such as our Sun. The Sun is 109 times the diameter of Earth and almost 333,000 times as heavy.

Earth may not be that big, but it is very special. It is the place that humans and other living things call home.

29

More Books about Earth

Earth and Beyond. Robert Snedden (Heinemann)

Earth and Universe. Storm Dunlop (Gareth Stevens)

Earth: The Third Planet. Michael D. Cole (Enslow)

Planet Earth. Kathryn Senior (Franklin Watts)

The Third Planet: Exploring the Earth from Space. Sally Ride and Tam O'Shaughnessy (Crown)

DVDs

Amazing Earth. (Artisan Entertainment)

Earthlight: NASA – Spectacular Views of Earth from Space. (DVD International)

Inside the Space Station. (Artisan Entertainment)

Mission to Mir. (Warner Home Video)

Web Sites

The Internet is a good place to get more information about Earth. The web sites listed here can help you learn about the most recent discoveries, as well as those made in the past.

Earth from Space. earth.jsc.nasa.gov/categories.html

Encyclopedia of the Atmospheric Environment. www.doc.mmu.ac.uk/aric/eae/english.html

International Space Station. spaceflight.nasa.gov/station/

Nine Planets. www.nineplanets.org/earth.html

U.S. Geological Survey. www.usgs.gov/

Views of the Solar System. www.solarviews.com/eng/earth.htm

Volcano World. volcano.und.nodak.edu/vw.html

Windows to the Universe. www.windows.ucar.edu/tour/link=/earth/earth.html

Places to Visit

Here are some museums and centers where you can find a variety of exhibits about Earth and space.

American Museum of Natural History
Central Park West at 79th Street
New York, NY 10024

Exploratorium
3601 Lyon Street
San Francisco, CA 94123

Henry Crown Space Center
Museum of Science and Industry
57th Street and Lake Shore Drive
Chicago, IL 60637

National Air and Space Museum
Smithsonian Institution
7th and Independence Avenue SW
Washington, DC 20560

Odyssium
11211 142nd Street
Edmonton, Alberta T5M 4A1
Canada

Glossary

atmosphere: the gases that surround a planet, star, or moon.

aurora: light at the North and South Poles of Earth caused by the collision of particles in the solar wind with Earth's atmosphere.

carbon dioxide: early in the history of our planet, one of the main gases, along with nitrogen, that made up Earth's atmosphere. When humans and animals breathe out, they exhale carbon dioxide.

core: the central part. The core of Earth is believed to consist mainly of iron and nickel.

craters: holes or pits on planets and moons created by the impact of meteorites or volcanic explosions.

crust: the outermost solid layer of a planet like Earth, including the surface area.

diameter: the distance across or the width of something.

evaporate: to change from a liquid into a vapor or a gas.

fault: a break, or crack, in Earth's crust often found where plates slide against each other.

ice ages: periods in the history of Earth that saw great ice glaciers cover parts of the land surface of the planet.

magnetic field: a field or area around a planet, such as Earth, where magnetic force can be felt. Many scientists believe that Earth's magnetic field is caused by the swirling of melted iron in Earth's core.

mantle: the hot, rocky matter that surrounds Earth's core and lies below the crust.

mass: a quantity, or amount, of matter.

orbit: the path that one celestial object follows as it circles, or revolves around, another.

oxygen: the gas in Earth's atmosphere that makes human and animal life possible.

ozone layer: a layer of Earth's atmosphere with a concentration of the gas ozone — a form of oxygen — that shields us from the Sun's dangerous ultraviolet light.

Pangea: the giant single continent that many scientists think made up the land surface of Earth hundreds of millions of years ago.

planet: one of the large bodies that revolve around a star like our Sun. Our Earth is one of the planets in our Solar System.

plates: sections of Earth's crust created by the movement of rock in Earth's mantle.

pole: either end of the axis around which a planet, moon, or star rotates.

Solar System: the Sun with the planets and all the other bodies, such as the asteroids, that orbit the Sun.

solar wind: tiny particles with an electric charge that travel from the Sun at a speed of hundreds of miles a second.

terraforming: a way of making a planet suitable for human life.

ultraviolet: a type of light whose wavelength is too short for it to be visible to the human eye.

Index

Born in 1920, Isaac Asimov came to the United States as a young boy from his native Russia. As a young man, he was a student of biochemistry. In time, he became one of the most productive writers the world has ever known. His books cover a spectrum of topics, including science, history, language theory, fantasy, and science fiction. His brilliant imagination gained him the respect and admiration of adults and children alike. Sadly, Isaac Asimov died shortly after the publication of the first edition of *Isaac Asimov's Library of the Universe.*

The publishers wish to thank the following for permission to reproduce copyright material: front cover, 3, NASA Goddard Space Flight Center; 4-5, 5, 6, © John Foster 1988; 7 (upper), © Lynette Cook 1988; 7 (center), National Space Science Data Center; 7 (lower right), © William Hartmann; 8 (upper), © Garret Moore 1988; 8 (lower), © Hachette Guides; 9, © Julian Baum 1988; 10, 11 (upper), NOAA; 11 (lower left), © 1995 Dave Bartruff; 11 (lower right), R. E. Wallace/USGS; 12, K. Jackson, U.S. Air Force; 13, K. Segerstrum/USGS; 14, © Garret Moore 1988; 15 (upper and inset), National Severe Storms Laboratory; 15 (lower), © Mark Maxwell 1988; 16 (upper), © Lynette Cook 1988; 16 (lower), © Forrest Baldwin; 17, © Forrest Baldwin; 18 (left), NASA and the Hubble Heritage Team (STScI/AURA); 18 (right, both), 19 (upper), NASA; 19 (lower), Jet Propulsion Laboratory; 20 (upper), © Tom Miller; 20 (lower left), © Chappell Studio; 20 (lower right), © Brian Parker/Tom Stack and Associates; 21, NASA Goddard Space Flight Center; 22 (left), U.S. Fish and Wildlife Service Photo by P. Martinkovic; 22 (right), © Dave Falzetti/Greenpeace; 23 (upper left), © Gary Milburn/Tom Stack and Associates; 23 (lower left), NASA; 23 (upper and lower right), © Rain Forest Action Network; 24-25, NASA Goddard Space Flight Center; 25 (left), NASA; 25 (right), NASA and Russian Space Agency; 26, © David A. Hardy 1988; 27, © Doug McLeod 1988; 28-29 (all), © Sally Bensusen 1988.